S0-CPD-433

MARTIN LUTHER KING JR.

BY RYAN NAGELHOUT

Gareth Stevens
PUBLISHING

Please visit our website, www.garethstevens.com. For a free color catalog of all our high-quality books, call toll free 1-800-542-2595 or fax 1-877-542-2596.

Library of Congress Cataloging-in-Publication Data

Nagelhout, Ryan.
Martin Luther King, Jr. / by Ryan Nagelhout.
p. cm. — (Heroes of black history)
Includes index.
ISBN 978-1-4824-2904-6 (pbk.)
ISBN 978-1-4824-2905-3 (6 pack)
ISBN 978-1-4824-2906-0 (library binding)
1. King, Martin Luther, Jr., 1929 - 1968 — Juvenile literature. 2. African Americans — Biography — Juvenile literature. 3. Civil rights workers — United States — Biography — Juvenile literature. I. Nagelhout, Ryan. II. Title.
E185.97.K5 N34 2016
323'.092—d23

First Edition

Published in 2016 by
Gareth Stevens Publishing
111 East 14th Street, Suite 349
New York, NY 10003

Copyright © 2016 Gareth Stevens Publishing

Designer: Katelyn E. Reynolds
Editor: Therese Shea

Photo credits: Cover, p. 1 Walter Bennett/The LIFE Picture Collection/Getty Images; cover, pp. 1–32 (background image) Photo Researchers/Science Source/Getty Images; pp. 5, 12, 19 Library of Congress Prints and Photographs Division Washington, DC 20540 USA; p. 7 Gary Conner/Photolibrary/Getty Images; p. 9 Prince Williams/Getty Images for Spelman College; p. 11 Donald Uhrbrock/The LIFE Picture Collection/Getty Images; p. 13 USIA/Wikipedia.org; pp. 15 (main), 21 Don Cravens/The LIFE Picture Collection/Getty Images; p. 15 (inset) BlackPast.org Blog; p. 16 Paul Schutzer/The LIFE Picture Collection/Getty Images; p. 17 Phil Greitzer/NY Daily News Archive/Getty Images; p. 23 AFP/Getty Images; p. 24 Keystone/Getty Images; p. 25 Cecil Stoughton, White House Press Office (WHPO)/Wikipedia.org; p. 27 (inset) Joseph Louw/The LIFE Picture Collection/Getty Images; p. 27 (main) Mondadori Portfolio/Getty Images; p. 28 Brendan Smialowski/AFP/Getty Images.

Printed in the United States of America

CPSIA compliance information: Batch #CS15GS: For further information contact Gareth Stevens, New York, New York at 1-800-542-2595.

CONTENTS

Words in the glossary appear in **bold** type the first time they are used in the text.

AN IMPORTANT MAN

When Martin Luther King Jr. was **assassinated** on April 4, 1968, in Memphis, Tennessee, a shocked world mourned. He was just 39, but King's work had made him into one of the most important people in American and world history.

Though King began as a smart but humble religious student and pastor, he assisted in building the American civil rights movement into an organized, effective group that inspired people of all races and faiths. Along with other civil rights leaders of the 1950s and 1960s, King helped millions of African Americans gain equal rights and forever changed the United States.

THE CHANGING TIMES

During King's life, inequality and racism—the belief that certain races of people are better than others—were common throughout the South and other parts of the United States. Though he lived just a few decades ago, the United States was a very different country than it is today. Life was much harder for most African Americans.

Martin Luther King Jr. was a gifted and powerful speaker,
a skill that helped him in his civil rights mission.

5

BORN A KING

Martin Luther King Jr. was born Michael King Jr. on January 15, 1929, in Atlanta, Georgia. King was the son, grandson, and great-grandson of Baptist ministers. King's father, Michael King, was a pastor, while his mother, Alberta Williams King, was a schoolteacher.

The first 12 years of King's life were spent at a home on Auburn Avenue with his parents and grandparents. The Kings lived in the Sweet Auburn neighborhood in Atlanta, a wealthy but **segregated** section of the city. Michael King Jr. grew up with older sister Christine and younger brother Alfred. In 1931, King's grandfather died, and his father became pastor of Ebenezer Baptist Church in Atlanta.

BECOMING MARTIN LUTHER

Michael King Jr.'s name changed after his father became inspired by a German religious reformer named Martin Luther (1483–1546). After taking a trip to Germany, Michael King Sr. decided to be known as Martin Luther King. His son's name changed to match. Michael King Jr.'s name was officially changed by law to "Martin Luther King Jr." in July 1957.

6

Today, King's childhood home on Auburn Avenue is a National Historic Site.

7

FINDING THE PATH

The Baptist faith was a major part of the King household. Young Michael King Jr. sang in the church choir when he was just 4. King was very intelligent. At Booker T. Washington High School, he skipped the ninth and twelfth grades. He began at Morehouse College in Atlanta when he was 15.

King considered studying medicine or law, but decided instead to follow in the footsteps of his father and grandfather. At 17, he preached his first **sermon** at his father's church. He was ordained, or appointed a minister, in his final year at Morehouse and graduated in 1948.

FINDING HIS VOICE

King's interest in social justice was sparked at Morehouse College, where he was taught that faith could produce change in the world. After a string of violence against African Americans, King wrote in a letter to the *Atlanta Constitution* newspaper that African Americans were "entitled to the basic rights and opportunities of American citizens."

IN MEMORY OF
MARTIN LUTHER KING. JR.[48]
1929 — 1968
OUTSTANDING ALUMNUS OF MOREHOUSE COLLEGE
WORLD-FAMOUS LEADER OF THE NON-VIOLENT MOVEMENT
DISTINGUISHED WINNER OF THE NOBEL PEACE PRIZE

From Morehouse College he launched his
humanitarian pilgrimage to create the
beloved community. and for that purpose
he moved out from the classroom and his
pulpit to march his way into immortality.

THIS STATUE IS A GIFT OF THE NATIONAL BAPTIST CONVENTION. U.S.A.,Inc.
T. J. JEMISON. PRESIDENT
W. FRANKLYN RICHARDSON. GENERAL SECRETARY
MOREHOUSE COLLEGE

Today, a bronze statue of King stands in front of the
Martin Luther King Jr. International Chapel at Morehouse College.

MAKING A FAMILY

After graduating from Morehouse, King studied at the Crozer Theological Seminary in Pennsylvania. Though he was just one of six African Americans to study theology there, he ~~popular~~ and was elected class president. In 1951, King ~~~~ at Boston University's School of Theology.

In Boston, King met Coretta Scott, a music major at the New England Conservatory of Music. The two married on June 18, 1953, in Marion, Alabama, at the Scott family home. The Kings later had four children: Yolanda, Martin Luther III, Dexter, and Bernice. Though she was busy caring for her family, Coretta Scott King took part in the budding civil rights movement, too.

BLOCKS EQUALITY

The issue of slavery put the United States through a civil war from 1861 to 1865, tearing the country in two. Even after the Thirteenth Amendment officially ended slavery in 1865, laws were passed to limit the rights of African Americans. These unfair "Jim Crow" laws were what King and other civil rights leaders fought against during the 1950s and 1960s.

Coretta Scott King and her children carried on King's **legacy** of peaceful protest after his death.

THE AWAKENING

In 1954, King accepted an offer to become the pastor of Dexter Avenue Baptist Church in Montgomery, Alabama. The Kings moved to the city and welcomed their first child, Yolanda, in November 1955.

On December 1, 1955, Rosa Parks was arrested on a Montgomery bus. She had refused to give up her seat to a white man, breaking one of the many Jim Crow laws in cities throughout the South. Parks's arrest challenged the lawfulness of the city's segregated bus system. Black leaders in the city created the Montgomery Improvement Association (MIA) and chose King as the MIA's head.

JIM CROW AT WORK

Jim Crow laws segregated restaurants, bathrooms, and even drinking fountains. In Georgia, one Jim Crow law even prevented blacks and whites from being buried in the same cemetery. King and other civil rights leaders fought to test the legality of these laws as well as bring attention to their unfairness.

After the victory in Montgomery, King helped found and was elected
president of the Southern Christian Leadership Conference (SCLC).

STABBED IN HARLEM

King saw his home bombed multiple times during the Montgomery bus boycott, but the first close attempt to assassinate him came in 1958. While signing copies of his book *Stride Toward Freedom* in New York City, King was stabbed with a letter opener 7 inches (18 cm) long. It hit close to his **aorta**. He had a 2-hour **surgery** to repair the wound.

SAVING KING'S LIFE

Dr. John Cordice and Dr. Emil Naclerio worked at Harlem Hospital, where King was taken after the stabbing. They were the two doctors of different races who performed King's surgery. Afterward, when King had fully recovered, he pointed to the teamwork of these doctors as an example of people working together to accomplish great things.

The doctors said that if King had even sneezed, he might have died.

His attacker was Izola Ware Curry, a 42-year-old woman who thought King and other black leaders were "boycotting" her and made her lose her job. The attack brought even more attention to the civil rights movement.

a supporter with King's book

King and his wife, Coretta, greet people from the steps of Harlem Hospital in 1958. Izola Curry was declared mentally unstable and didn't face trial for the attack. King later said he held no anger toward her.

ALWAYS WATCHING

Despite King's efforts to peacefully protest and work for civil rights, not everyone believed in his cause or trusted his methods. King and his family received countless death threats, but even people in the federal government were unsure he could be trusted. Federal Bureau of Investigation (FBI) chief J. Edgar Hoover had King under surveillance, or close watch. The FBI recorded his phone conversations and kept track of his movements.

There's also proof the FBI tried to make black leaders distrust King by leaking information about him to them. King even thought Hoover sent him a letter in the hope that King would kill himself.

HOOVER VS. KING

King was suspicious of the many threats he received and thought a number of them were from Hoover and the FBI. Hoover did little to hide his dislike of King. In 1964, Hoover called King "the most **notorious** liar in the country" at a Washington press conference. King replied that Hoover must be "under extreme pressure" to make such a statement.

J. Edgar Hoover

A decade later, a Senate committee proved that a threatening letter sent to King came from the FBI. This kind of activity made many wonder if the government was involved in King's death.

19

MOVING FORWARD

King continued to fight for improved rights for African Americans in the South after the success of the Montgomery bus boycott. He traveled throughout the southern states helping organize people, giving speeches, and carrying out protests. A major campaign began in Birmingham, Alabama, in 1963. TV news cameras showed the nation what was happening there, including police using high-pressure fire hoses and attack dogs against peaceful protesters.

King was arrested for leading a protest in Birmingham. He wrote his "Letter from Birmingham Jail" there, arguing that people should break unjust laws. By 1963, King started to organize a groundbreaking march on Washington, DC.

MORE THAN CIVIL RIGHTS

King spoke out against a variety of topics beyond the quest for equal rights for African Americans. He was active in the fight against poor conditions in black neighborhoods in Chicago, Illinois, even moving his family there briefly. King's nonviolent beliefs also extended to military conflicts. He spoke out against US involvement in the Vietnam War (1954–1975).

Coretta Scott King recalled her husband was arrested 29 times during protests and marches for civil rights.

21

THE DREAM DEFINED

On August 28, 1963, the American civil rights movement reached an important moment with the March on Washington for Jobs and Freedom. More than 250,000 people attended the march, flooding Washington, DC, to hear Martin Luther King Jr. deliver one of the most famous speeches in American history. King said, "I have a dream that one day this nation will rise up and live out the true meaning of its **creed**: 'We hold these truths to be **self-evident**: that all men are created equal.'" The 16-minute speech laid out his vision for the future of the United States, when people of all races could live together in peace.

MALCOLM VS. MARTIN

Not all African American leaders believed in King's methods. Unlike King, Malcolm X, another civil rights champion of the 1960s, didn't dismiss violence as a way to gain more rights. For a time, he also thought white people couldn't help or understand the African American struggle for civil rights. Malcolm X, too, was assassinated for his work.

The speech was heard on the radio and viewed on television by millions around the world. King called the March on Washington "the greatest **demonstration** of freedom in the history of the United States."

23

ACTING AT LAST

Nearly a century after the passing of the Thirteenth Amendment, the Civil Rights Act of 1964 outlawed unfair treatment of people based on their race, skin color, and other features or beliefs. King had fought for years for such a law and had been arrested and beaten countless times for it. He was in the room when President Lyndon Johnson signed the act into law.

Another important civil rights moment came in 1965 with the passage of the Voting Rights Act. It removed many of the laws that made it hard for people of color to cast votes in elections.

YOUNG PEACEMAKER

In 1964, 35-year-old Martin Luther King Jr. won the Nobel Peace Prize for his leadership role in the nonviolent civil rights movement. He accepted the award but gave the prize money, about $54,000, to civil rights causes. King was the youngest person to win the prize until 2014, when 17-year-old Malala Yousafzai of Pakistan was awarded the honor. ▶

President John Kennedy had introduced the idea of a national civil rights act. However, he was assassinated in Texas in 1963 before it came to pass.

25

SHOTS IN MEMPHIS

On April 4, 1968, Martin Luther King Jr. was in Memphis, Tennessee, supporting garbage workers' rights. While standing outside of room 306 of the Lorraine Hotel, King was shot in the head. The civil rights leader was rushed to the hospital, where he died. President Johnson called for a national day of mourning on April 7.

King's funeral was held 2 days later in Atlanta, Georgia.

King was buried near Ebenezer Baptist Church, where he first started his ministry all those years ago. His family worked to establish the King Center in Atlanta to further his goals and the struggle against inequality.

MORE TRAGEDY

Six years after Martin Luther King Jr.'s assassination, Alberta Williams King, his 70-year-old mother, was killed by a gunman at Ebenezer Baptist Church in Atlanta. At the time, she was playing the organ during a morning service. The gunman, Marcus Wayne Chenault Jr., was sentenced to death. However, the King family requested life in prison instead.

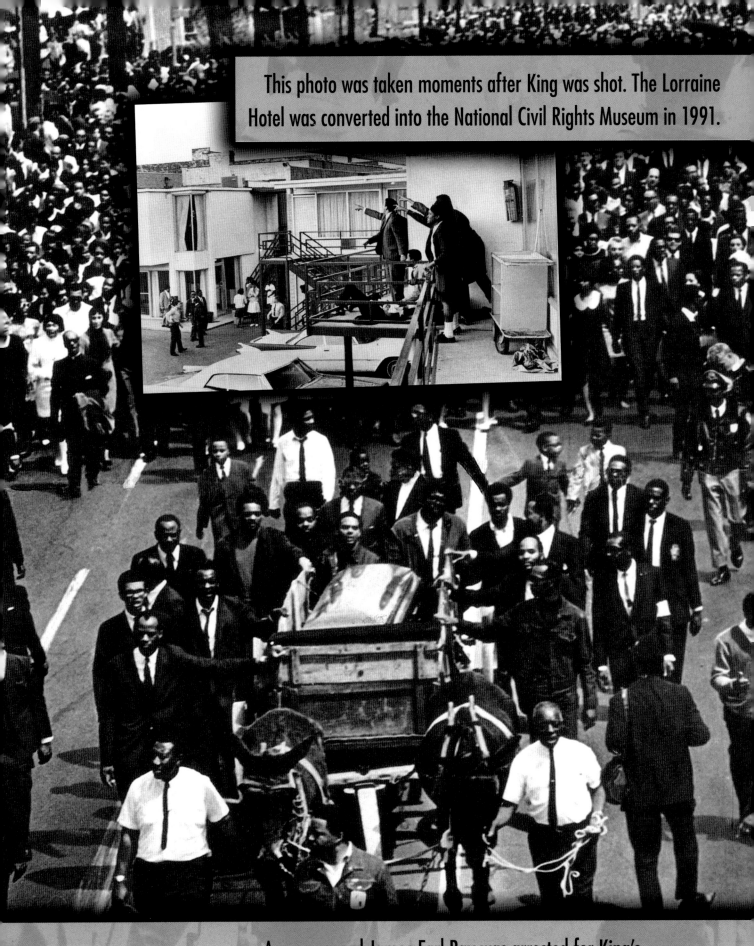

This photo was taken moments after King was shot. The Lorraine Hotel was converted into the National Civil Rights Museum in 1991.

A man named James Earl Ray was arrested for King's assassination in June 1968, about 2 months after King's funeral. The funeral procession is shown here.

27

REMEMBERING A KING

In 1983, Martin Luther King Jr. Day became a national holiday. Every third Monday in January is set aside to remember King's legacy of peace and service to others.

On August 28, 2011, the Martin Luther King Jr. Memorial opened on the National Mall in Washington, DC, 48 years after the March on Washington. The white granite sculpture of King is 30 feet (9.1 m) tall. It's a towering reminder of his life, work, and sacrifice for the rights of all people, both in the United States and around the world.

KING ACROSS THE GLOBE

Martin Luther King Jr.'s work changed life in the United States, but it was noticed throughout the world, too. His likeness can be seen in places other than the United States. There's a statue of King in Westminster Abbey in London, England, and even a Martin Luther King Street in Jerusalem in the Middle East!

MARTIN LUTHER KING JR.: A TIMELINE OF HIS LIFE

1929 — Martin Luther King Jr. is born Michael King Jr. on January 15.

1944 — Martin attends Morehouse College at age 15.

1948 — King graduates from Morehouse College.

1953 — King marries Coretta Scott on June 18.

1954 — King becomes pastor of Dexter Avenue Baptist Church in Montgomery, Alabama.

1955 — Martin Luther King Jr. leads the Montgomery bus boycott.

1957 — King's name is legally changed to Martin Luther King Jr.

1963 — King delivers the "I Have a Dream" speech in Washington, DC.

1964 — The Civil Rights Act is passed. King wins the Nobel Peace Prize.

1965 — The Voting Rights Act is passed.

1968 — King is assassinated in Memphis, Tennessee, on April 4.

2011 — The Martin Luther King Jr. Memorial opens on the National Mall.

GLOSSARY

aorta: the main artery, or blood vessel, that carries blood from the heart to the rest of the body

assassinate: to kill someone, especially a public figure

boycott: the act of refusing to have dealings with a person or business in order to force change

car pool: a group of people who share a car when they are going to and from places

creed: an idea or set of beliefs that guides the actions of a person or group

demonstration: an event in which people gather together in order to show that they support or oppose something or someone

legacy: something that is passed down to someone

notorious: well-known or famous, especially for something bad

segregated: separated according to race by force

self-evident: clearly true and requiring no proof or explanation

sermon: a speech about a subject that is usually given by a religious leader

surgery: medical treatment in which a doctor cuts into someone's body in order to repair or remove damaged or diseased parts

unconstitutional: not allowed by a country's constitution, which is the highest law

FOR MORE INFORMATION

BOOKS

Aretha, David. *Martin Luther King Jr. and the 1963 March on Washington.* Greensboro, NC: Morgan Reynolds Publishing, 2013.

Herrington, Lisa M. *Martin Luther King Jr. Day.* New York, NY: Children's Press, 2013.

Schwartz, Heather E. *The March on Washington: A Primary Source Exploration of the Pivotal Protest.* North Mankato, MN: Capstone Press, 2015.

WEBSITES

The King Center Archive
thekingcenter.org/archive
Look at papers, photos, and more at the King Center.

Martin Luther King Jr.'s Nobel Prize Page
nobelprize.org/nobel_prizes/peace/laureates/1964/king-bio.html
Find out more about Martin Luther King Jr.'s accomplishments on this site.

Martin Luther King's Speech: 'I Have a Dream'
www.americanrhetoric.com/speeches/mlkihaveadream.htm
Read the full text of Martin Luther King Jr.'s famous 1963 speech.

INDEX